AF270640

Stellar Space

# SpaceX

by Julie Murray



Dash!
LEVELED READERS
An Imprint of Abdo Zoom • abdobooks.com

3

### Level 1 – Beginning
Short and simple sentences with familiar words or patterns for children who are beginning to understand how letters and sounds go together.

### Level 2 – Emerging
Longer words and sentences with more complex language patterns for readers who are practicing common words and letter sounds.

### Level 3 – Transitional
More developed language and vocabulary for readers who are becoming more independent.

## abdobooks.com

Published by Abdo Zoom, a division of ABDO, PO Box 398166, Minneapolis, Minnesota 55439. Copyright © 2022 by Abdo Consulting Group, Inc. International copyrights reserved in all countries. No part of this book may be reproduced in any form without written permission from the publisher. Dash!™ is a trademark and logo of Abdo Zoom.

Printed in the United States of America, North Mankato, Minnesota.
052021
092021

Photo Credits: Alamy, Getty Images, iStock, NASA, Shutterstock
Production Contributors: Kenny Abdo, Jennie Forsberg, Grace Hansen, John Hansen
Design Contributors: Candice Keimig, Neil Klinepier, Victoria Bates

## Library of Congress Control Number: 2020919705

## Publisher's Cataloging in Publication Data

Names: Murray, Julie, author.
Title: SpaceX / by Julie Murray
Description: Minneapolis, Minnesota : Abdo Zoom, 2022 | Series: Stellar space | Includes online resources and index.
Identifiers: ISBN 9781098226299 (lib. bdg.) | ISBN 9781098226435 (ebook) | ISBN 9781098226503 (Read-to-Me ebook)
Subjects: LCSH: Outer space--Juvenile literature. | SpaceX (Firm)--Juvenile literature. | Space colonies--Juvenile literature. | Space launch industry--Juvenile literature. | Launch vehicles (Astronautics)--Juvenile literature.
Classification: DDC 629.41--dc23

# Table of Contents

# The Beginning

SpaceX is an American aerospace company. Its full name is Space Exploration Technologies Corporation. Elon Musk founded the company in 2002.

SpaceX designs, **manufactures**, and launches rockets. The rockets are designed to be reused, something that has never been done before.

SpaceX launches **satellites** too. It is also a space transportation service, helping to haul cargo and astronauts to the **International Space Station (ISS)**.

# Missions

SpaceX's Falcon 1 launched on September 28, 2008. It was the first **private** liquid-fueled vehicle to go into **orbit** around the Earth.

SPACEX
12

Falcon Heavy is a heavy-lift launch vehicle. It ran a test flight in February 2018. It carried a Tesla Roadster car into space. A dummy named "Starman" was in the driver's seat. The launch was a success!

In 2019, SpaceX began launching Starlink **satellites**. The small satellites link together and communicate with ground **transceivers**. This brings people internet access from space!

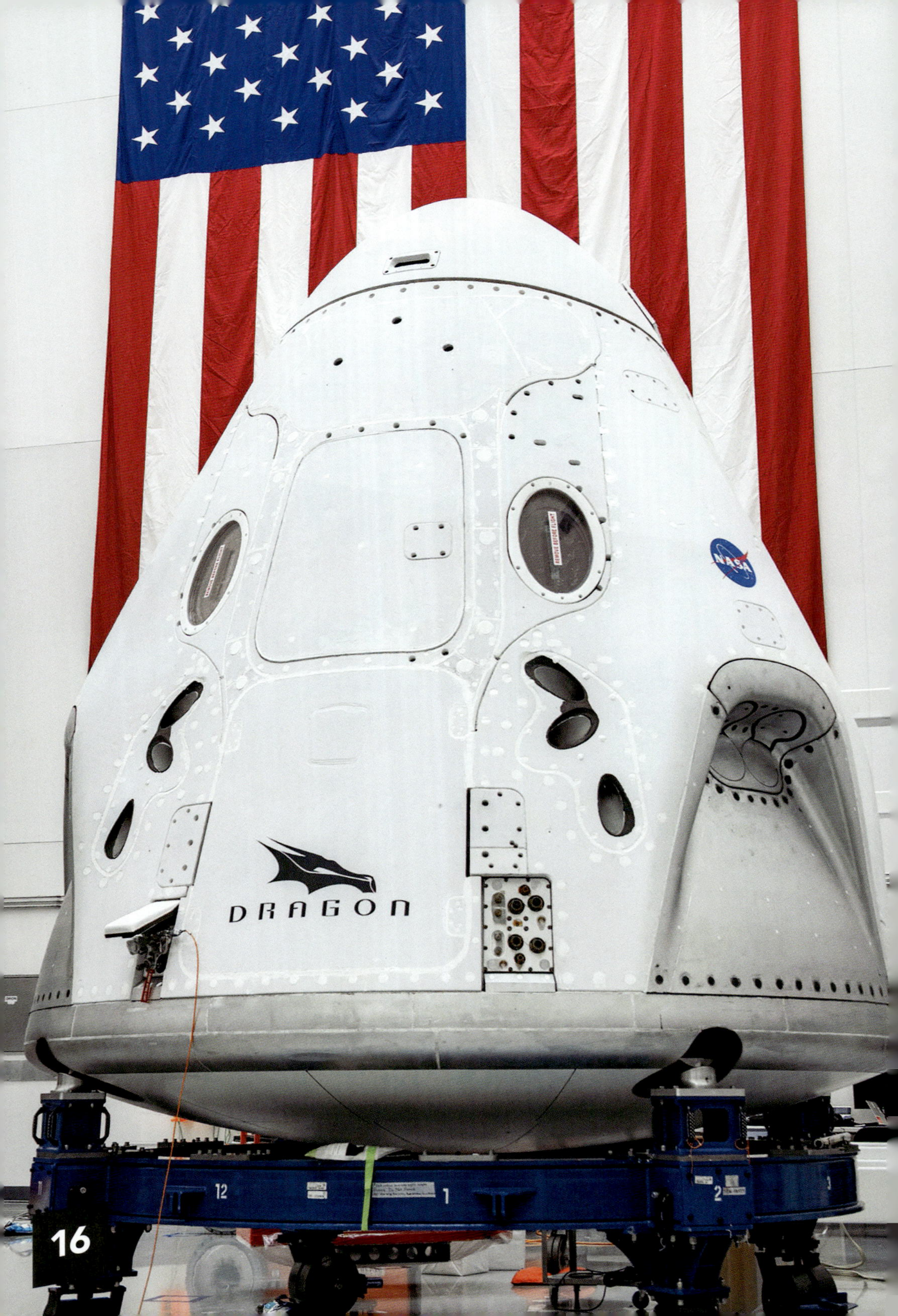

Dragon spacecrafts carry cargo and passengers into space. They have been hauling cargo to the **ISS** since 2012. Crew Dragon became the first **private** spacecraft to take humans to the ISS in 2020.

# Looking to the Future

SpaceX's Starship is designed for long-duration cargo hauls through space. It is reusable and extremely powerful. Starship will eventually carry passengers.

SpaceX is looking to the future of spaceflight. It hopes to one day transport people and equipment to the moon and Mars!

# SpaceX Facts

- Headquartered in Hawthorne, California

- Employs about 8,000 people

- First to launch a privately built spacecraft into orbit and return it safely to Earth

- Provides high-speed internet to rural areas in the United States through Starlink

- Falcon 1 was the world's first orbital class reusable rocket

- Falcon Heavy has 27 engines with 5 million pounds of thrust at takeoff

- Dragon spacecrafts have flown over 20 missions to the **ISS**

# Glossary

**International Space Station (ISS)** – a large spacecraft in orbit around Earth. It serves as a home and science laboratory where crews of astronauts live and work. Several nations worked together to build it.

**manufacture** – to make by machine in large quantities.

**orbit** – (n) the curved path in which a natural or artificial body moves in a circle around a star, planet, or moon. (v) to move in a circle around.

**private** – not owned by the government.

**satellite** – a spacecraft that is sent into orbit around a planet or other heavenly body in order to collect information.

**transceiver** – a device that is able to both transmit and receive information.

# Index



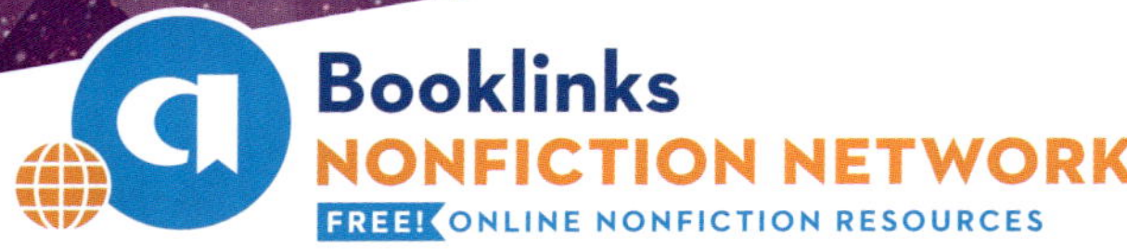

# Online Resources

**Booklinks**
**NONFICTION NETWORK**
**FREE!** ONLINE NONFICTION RESOURCES

To learn more about SpaceX, please visit **abdobooklinks.com** or scan this QR code. These links are routinely monitored and updated to provide the most current information available.